TIME
FOR KIDS
BOOK OF WHAT

EVERYTHING
SPACE

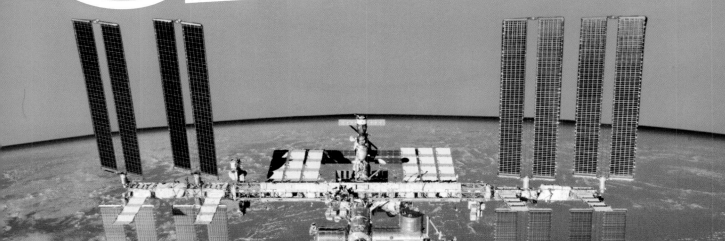

TIME FOR KIDS

Managing Editor, TIME For Kids: Nellie Gonzalez Cutler
Editor, Time Learning Ventures: Jonathan Rosenbloom

Book Packager: R studio T, New York City
Art Direction/Design: Raúl Rodriguez and Rebecca Tachna
Writer: Catherine Nichols
Illustrator: Chris Reed
Photo Researchers: Miriam Budnick, Elizabeth Vezzulla
Designers: Fabian Contreras, Ames Montgomery
Copyeditor: Joe Bomba
Indexer: Charles Karchmer
Fact Checkers: Luis Pereyra, Audrey Whitley

Redesign: Downtown Bookworks, Inc.
Project Manager: Sara DiSalvo

Cover: Symbology Creative

TIME INC. BOOKS

Publisher: Margot Schupf
Vice President, Finance: Vandana Patel
Executive Director, Marketing Services: Carol Pittard
Executive Director, Business Development: Suzanne Albert
Executive Director, Marketing: Susan Hettleman
Publishing Director: Megan Pearlman
Associate Director of Publicity: Courtney Greenhalgh
Assistant General Counsel: Simone Procas
Assistant Director, Special Sales: Ilene Schreider
Assistant Director, Finance: Christine Font
Senior Manager, Sales Marketing: Danielle Costa
Senior Manager, Children's Category Marketing: Amanda Lipnick
Associate Production Manager: Amy Mangus
Associate Prepress Manager: Alex Voznesenskiy
Associate Project Manager: Stephanie Braga

Editorial Director: Stephen Koepp
Art Director: Gary Stewart
Senior Editors: Roe D'Angelo, Alyssa Smith
Managing Editor: Matt DeMazza
Editor, Children's Books: Jonathan White
Copy Chief: Rina Bander
Design Manager: Anne-Michelle Gallero
Assistant Managing Editor: Gina Scauzillo
Editorial Assistant: Courtney Mifsud

Special thanks: Allyson Angle, Keith Aurelio, Katherine Barnet, Brad Beatson, Jeremy Biloon, John Champlin, Ian Chin, Susan Chodakiewicz, Rose Cirrincione, Assu Etsubneh, Mariana Evans, Alison Foster, Kristina Jutzi, David Kahn, Jean Kennedy, Hillary Leary, Samantha Long, Kimberly Marshall, Robert Martells, Nina Mistry, Melissa Presti, Danielle Prielipp, Babette Ross, Dave Rozzelle, Matthew Ryan, Ricardo Santiago, Divyam Shrivastava

Contents of this book previously appeared in TIME FOR KIDS Big Book of WHAT.

For information on TIME FOR KIDS magazine for the classroom or home, go to TIMEFORKIDS.COM or call 800-777-8600. For subscriptions to SI KIDS, go to SIKIDS.COM or call 800-889-6007.

Published by TIME FOR KIDS Books,
An imprint of Time Inc. Books
1271 Avenue of the Americas, 6th floor
New York, NY 10020

ISBN 10: 1-61893-390-6
ISBN 13: 978-1-61893-390-4

TIME FOR KIDS is a trademark of Time Inc.

We welcome your comments and suggestions about TIME FOR KIDS Books. Please write to us at: TIME FOR KIDS Books, Attention: Book Editors, P.O. Box 361095, Des Moines, IA 50336-1095
If you would like to order any of our hardcover Collector's Edition books, please call us at 800-327-6388 (Monday through Friday, 7 a.m.–9 p.m. Central Time).

1 QGT 15

Contents

WHAT Is the Biggest Known Star in the Universe?

Stars come in many sizes, from small dwarfs to supergiants. Our sun is an average-size star, 870,000 miles across and big enough that one million Earths could comfortably fit inside it. But that's nothing compared to the biggest known star in the universe. VY Canis Majoris, a red supergiant with a diameter of more than 1.7 billion miles, is roughly 2,100 times the size of the sun in radius and could swallow it 8 billion times over.

A Dying Star

Images from the Hubble Space Telescope reveal that VY Canis Majoris is about to burn up. That's not too surprising since supergiants, the most massive of stars, send out energy at a much higher rate than smaller stars. While our sun will shine for about 10 billion years, supergiants last only a few million. When a supergiant finally runs out of fuel, it explodes, becoming a supernova.

Don't hold your breath waiting for VY Canis Majoris to blow up, though. Astronomers believe that probably won't happen for another 100,000 years or so. In human years that seems like a long time, but in astronomical years, it's a blink of an eye.

As it nears the end of its life, VY Canis Majoris puts out so much radiation that parts of its outer layers are thrown off in large outbursts. These two images, taken by the Hubble Space Telescope, show such an eruption.

Every day, scientists learn new facts about our solar system—and beyond. So fasten your seatbelts and get ready to explore the farthest reaches of the universe.

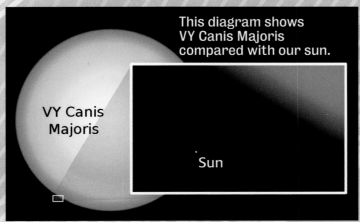

This diagram shows VY Canis Majoris compared with our sun.

VY Canis Majoris

Sun

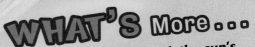

WHAT'S More...

○ If VY Canis Majoris took the sun's place in our solar system, its surface would extend out to Saturn's orbit.

○ VY Canis Majoris is also a hypergiant, a star that is both massive and bright. It is about 450,000 times brighter than the sun.

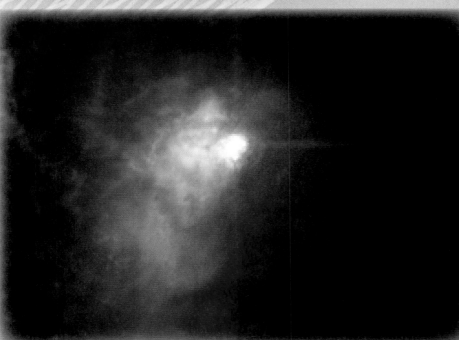

WHAT Is the Dark Part of Space Made Of?

If you took all the stars, planets, and galaxies and combined them, they would make up just 4% of the universe. So what about the other 96%? The dark part of space consists of two things: dark energy and dark matter. Neither can be seen, at least not with the technology we have today. So how do scientists know they exist? Scientists figured out dark energy and dark matter are real when they studied the effects of gravity on the objects in space that we can see, such as stars and galaxies.

Dark Matter: The Glue that Holds the Universe Together

In 1933, Swiss astronomer Fritz Zwicky studied the Coma galaxy cluster and became the first to suspect that dark matter existed. He compared the galaxy's mass to its gravitational pull and noticed that the numbers weren't adding up. The combined mass of all visible matter wasn't enough to explain the force needed to hold the galaxy together. Zwicky reasoned that another kind of matter had to be at work—what he called dark matter.

The Hubble Space Telescope photographed the Coma cluster of galaxies (above) and a spiral galaxy (right)

The Milky Way as seen from Earth (above) and from NASA's Chandra X-ray Observatory (right)

It wasn't until 40 or so years later that scientists found more evidence that dark matter existed. In the 1970s, American astronomer Vera Rubin studied the Milky Way and other spiral galaxies. She observed that the stars in the galaxies were spinning in surprising ways, moving at a quicker speed that defied the rules of physics. She and other scientists came to believe that dark matter was providing extra gravity that caused the stars to travel so fast.

Dark Energy: Anti-Gravity

Dark energy, which makes up about 74% of the universe, is stretching the universe apart. Scientists have long known that the universe is getting bigger, with many galaxies moving farther and farther away from each other. Then in 1998, experiments showed that the rate of expansion was speeding up. Astronomers concluded that dark energy was pulling bits of matter apart. Gravity is a force that pulls objects closer. Dark energy, then, is gravity's opposite.

WHAT Is the Hottest Planet in Our Solar System?

A good guess might be Mercury, since it is the planet closest to the sun. But the correct answer is the next closest, Venus. Known as Earth's twin, Venus is similar to our planet in many ways. Both are about the same size, both have cloudy atmospheres, and both share some of the same landscape features: mountains, plains, and high plateaus. But while Earth has an average temperature of 57°F, Venus averages a scorching 863°F. What's more, the temperature on Venus remains constant all over the planet, and it's as hot at night as it is during the day.

Why Is Venus So Hot?

The answer lies in its thick atmosphere, the densest in our solar system. Thick yellow clouds made up of carbon dioxide blanket the planet. The clouds trap the sun's heat in Venus's atmosphere, so the planet is always hot. Many scientists believe that Venus once had oceans, just like Earth, but they evaporated.

The clouds covering Venus hide its desertlike surface.

WHAT'S More...

After our moon, Venus is the brightest object in the night sky.

WHAT Is the Only Planet in Our Solar System that Rotates on Its Side?

All the planets are tilted, but none compare to Uranus. The seventh planet from the sun has a 98-degree tilt to its axis so it rotates on its side. Instead of spinning like a top around the sun the way the other planets do, Uranus looks like a rolling ball.

What happened to make Uranus so different? Many astronomers suspect that billions of years ago something big crashed into Uranus and knocked it on its side. Another theory has to do with gravitational pull. Back when our solar system was new, the pull of gravity from other large planets might have knocked Uranus on its side.

Rotating sideways has had a big effect on the planet's seasons. Uranus orbits the sun once every 84 years. That means when its north pole points to the sun, the northern hemisphere has 42 years of sunlight. Then, it's the southern hemisphere's turn for summer and the northern side spends the next 42 years in darkness.

WHAT'S More . . .

Voyager 2 is the only spacecraft to have visited Uranus. In January 1986, it flew past the icy planet, taking thousands of photos of the planet, its 27 moons, and its rings (left).

This illustration shows some of Uranus's rings and its sideways rotation.

WHAT Is the Largest Moon in Our Solar System?

It's fitting that the largest moon in our solar system orbits the largest planet. Ganymede measures 3,270 miles in diameter and is so big that if it orbited the sun instead of Jupiter, astronomers would classify it as a planet.

The seventh moon from Jupiter, Ganymede is larger than Mercury and one-third the size of Earth. It's named after a boy from Greek mythology who became a servant to the gods. The astronomer Galileo Galilei discovered Ganymede in 1610, along with three other moons of Jupiter. He saw the four moons for the first time through a telescope he made himself.

Ganymede's outer layer is made up of ice and rock. Scientists think it's likely that a vast ocean lies more than 100 miles below the surface.

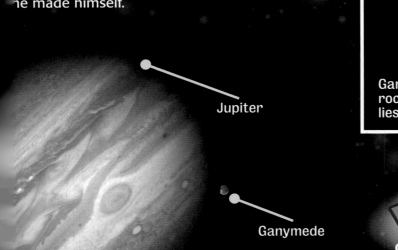

Jupiter

Ganymede

WHAT'S More . . .

Ganymede is one of Jupiter's 63 moons. The planet has more moons than any other in our solar system.

WHAT Is the Difference Between a Comet and an Asteroid?

Both comets and asteroids are relatively small objects that orbit the sun and were formed in the early days of our solar system. But there the likeness ends. Comets, often called dirty snowballs, are made up primarily of ice with dust and rock particles mixed in. When comets draw closer to the sun, they begin to vaporize, and a halo, called a coma, forms around them. High-speed solar winds produce the long tails that give comets their distinctive look.

Asteroids come in all shapes and sizes and are composed of rock and metal, leftover scraps from when the solar system formed. Most asteroids orbit in the asteroid belt between Mars and Jupiter.

The photos of two different comets were taken by NASA spacecrafts.

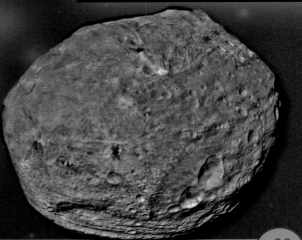

An artist created a picture of an asteroid (above). The photo of another asteroid, called Vesta, was taken by NASA (right).

WHAT Is an Orrery?

An orrery (*awr*-uh-ree) is a mechanical model of the solar system that shows the positions and motions of the planets and their moons. Orreries became popular in the 17th and 18th centuries, a time when educated people became very interested in science. Then and now, people use orreries to demonstrate how the planets orbit around the sun. One early example was made for an English nobleman, the Earl of Orrery, which is how the model got its name.

Not all orreries include every one of the planets. The sun always sits in the center, but the number of planets going around it can vary. Earth usually appears, as do Mercury, Venus, Mars, and Jupiter. Some orreries include all the planets, plus some of their moons as well. Most aren't built to scale, but all the machines correctly show how the planets orbit the sun.

This painting from 1766 shows a man explaining how an orrery works.

This orrery was built in 1773. It includes all the planets that were known at the time—Mercury, Venus, Earth, Mars, Jupiter, and Saturn.

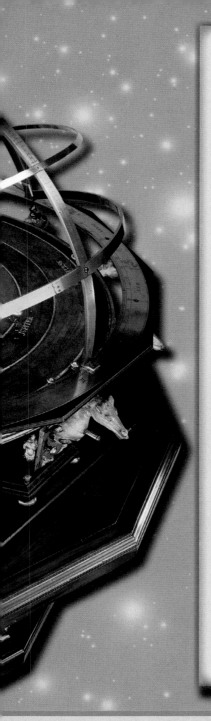

A Modern Orrery

You can see this orrery, called the Long Now, in a small museum in San Francisco, California. The model is eight feet high and shows the positions of the planets through Saturn. The orrery moves twice a day. It will take Earth 365 days to travel around the stationary sun, the same amount of time as the actual planet.

Human Orrery

In some orreries, the only moving parts are people. A famous human orrery takes place in Ireland's Armagh Observatory. On the observatory's grounds, people can stand on steel disks that mark the orbits of planets, a dwarf planet, and two comets. As visitors "orbit" the sun, they learn how the solar system works.

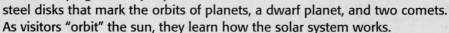

WHAT Is a Solar Eclipse?

Before people understood what caused a solar eclipse, they feared them. In Asia, people believed that a dragon in the sky was swallowing the sun. To scare it away, Chinese people banged on pots and pans. It worked! The sun always reappeared.

Today, we know that a solar eclipse occurs when the moon is in its new phase—the stage when the shaded portion of the moon faces the Earth—and moves in front of the sun. Since the Earth, the moon, and the sun must line up in a straight line for this to happen, solar eclipses are rare.

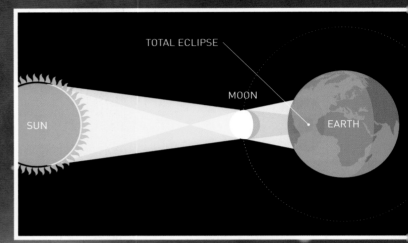

TOTAL ECLIPSE

MOON

SUN

EARTH

As the moon creeps past the sun, the sun gradually disappears. Eventually just a small part shows. Astronomers call this the diamond ring effect. Can you guess why?

This girl uses special glasses to watch a solar eclipse. The glasses filter out harmful rays that can cause eye damage. Never look directly at the sun, not even during a solar eclipse.

Create a Solar Eclipse

What You Need

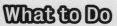

- straw
- scissors
- quarter
- orange
- flashlight

What to Do

1. Cut a slit in the straw and insert the coin.

2. If you're a righty, hold the straw in your right hand, pick up the orange with your left hand. If you're a lefty, do the opposite.

3. Position the two objects in a line about eight inches apart.

4. Ask a friend or family member to shine the flashlight from behind the quarter.

5. Observe the shadow the coin (moon) casts on the orange (Earth).

6. Note how the coin blocks the light and casts a shadow on the orange. The darker central shadow, the umbra, shows a total eclipse. The lighter outer area, the penumbra, shows a partial eclipse.

WHAT'S More . . .

Sometimes the Earth moves directly between the sun and the moon. When this happens, it's called a lunar eclipse.

WHAT Is a Blue Moon?

A blue moon isn't blue at all. It's the name given to the second full moon in a calendar month. Two full moons in one month don't happen all that often. Most years have 12 full moons, one appearing each month. But once every three years or so, an extra full moon slips in. That's because our calendar is based on the amount of time it takes Earth to orbit the sun and not on the lunar month, which is 29½ days.

This definition of a blue moon is a modern one and it came about by mistake. Before 1946, the *Farmers' Almanac* said a blue moon was the third full moon in a season that has four full moons. A writer for an astronomy magazine misunderstood the meaning and wrote that a blue moon was the second full moon in a month. This meaning stuck. In 1999, the error was discovered. But since more than 50 years had passed, most people continue to call the second moon in a month a blue moon.

WHAT'S More . . .

The expression "once in a blue moon" means something that happens rarely, just like two full moons in one month.

Full Moon Names

Many cultures around the world gave names to each month's full moon. Here are the names from North America's Algonquin tribes. European settlers later adopted many of the names.

MONTH	FULL MOON NAME
January	Wolf Moon
February	Snow Moon
March	Worm Moon
April	Pink Moon
May	Flower Moon
June	Strawberry Moon
July	Buck Moon
August	Sturgeon Moon
September	Harvest Moon
October	Hunter's Moon
November	Beaver Moon
December	Cold Moon

WHAT Is Earth's Larges[t] [M]eteorite?

[In 193]0, a farmer was turning over the soil in a field in Namibia, in southwestern Africa, [when] his plow hit an obstacle. When it was dug up, the large mass of metal turned out to [be the] largest meteorite ever found. The Hoba meteorite, named after the farm where it w[as discov]ered, weighs more than 60 tons. It is about nine feet long, nine feet wide, and thre[e feet thick.] It's 84% iron and 16% nickel, with trace amounts of other metals. Scientists estima[te it fell] [in]to Earth around 80,000 years ago.

[Run]ner-Up

[The Ca]pe York meteorite is the world's second largest, weighing in [at 34 t]ons. It hit Earth some 10,000 years ago, landing in Greenland. [Robert] Peary, the famous Arctic explorer, discovered the meteorite [in 189]4. Like the Hoba, the Cape York is made up of iron and nickel. [Unlike] the Hoba, it didn't stay where it landed. Peary hauled the big [chunk] of metal to New York City. You can see—and touch—it at the [Americ]an Museum of Natural History.

Robert P[eary]

WHAT Was the Space Shuttle?

From TIME FOR KIDS

Thirty years ago, space travel was far from routine. Back then, only a handful of Americans had traveled to space, and they had done so on spacecraft that could only be used once. At the end of the voyage, the crafts would parachute into the ocean, never to be flown again.

All of that changed when NASA rolled out its first space shuttle in 1981. The new spacecraft was designed to blast off using rocket boosters, orbit the Earth, and land like a plane—over and over again.

Shuttle Highs and Lows

In the last 30 years, NASA's five shuttles have completed more than 130 missions. They have helped the agency achieve many goals, from launching flying telescopes to helping to build the International Space Station (ISS), a floating space lab in the sky. The program has also seen its share of darker days. Fourteen lives were tragically lost in two shuttle accidents. After each disaster, NASA paused the shuttle program.

1980

SHUTTLE HISTORY

Here are some of the most important events in the shuttle's past.

April 12, 1981
The first shuttle craft, *Columbia*, lifts off, carrying two astronauts.

June 18, 1983
Challenger sails into orbit with Sally Ride. She is the first U.S. woman in space. Two months later, Guion Bluford becomes the first African American to travel into space.

February 7, 1984
An untethered astronaut spacewalks for the first time.

January 28, 1986
Seven crew members lose their lives when *Challenger* explodes shortly after liftoff. NASA suspends flights for nearly three years.

1990

April 24, 1990
Discovery launches the Hubble Space Telescope. Scientists soon realize that there is a defect in Hubble's main mirror, causing pictures to come out blurry.

The *Endeavour* is one of the five shuttles retired from the space program.

The End of an Era

On July 21, 2011, the space shuttle *Atlantis* concluded its final mission, marking the end of the space shuttle program. The U.S. government says the space vehicles are too old and too costly to operate. Instead of soaring into space, the shuttles will be on display in museums. And NASA astronauts will be left without a ride of their own. For now, to reach ISS, they will have to pay to travel aboard Russian spacecraft. Due to recent budget cuts in the space program, NASA scientists suspect that U.S. astronauts might be hitchhiking to space for some time.

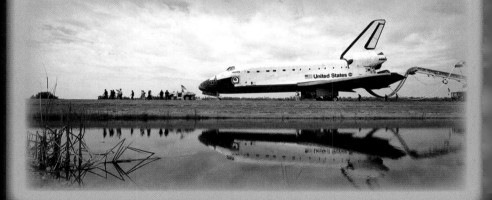

2000

2010

December 2, 1993
Endeavour takes a crew to repair Hubble's mirror. After days of work, Hubble is fixed.

October 29, 1998
John Glenn, who in 1962 became the first American to orbit Earth, returns to space aboard *Discovery*. At 77, he is the oldest space traveler.

December 6, 1998
Endeavour delivers the first U.S. piece of the International Space Station.

February 1, 2003
Seven astronauts lose their lives as *Columbia* returns to Earth. The shuttle breaks apart minutes before it is expected to land. NASA suspends flights for more than two years.

July 21, 2011
Atlantis completes its final mission. NASA retires its shuttle program.

WHAT Is a Space Probe?

Thanks to space probes, we know a lot more about space than ever before. Space probes are unmanned spacecraft that explore the solar system, taking detailed photos and gathering information about heavenly bodies. Space probes might fly past planets, orbit around them, or land on them. Once a probe is inside the planet's atmosphere or has landed, instruments on board conduct experiments. The information is then relayed back to Earth for scientists to study.

A Viking lander on Mars

Mars Touchdowns

The first probe to successfully land on Mars touched down in 1976. The two Viking landers relayed to Earth the first color images of the planet's rusty surface. The landers also scooped up soil samples and tested them for evidence of life forms. The results came back negative, but scientists are hopeful that future probes might prove different.

In 2004, twin rovers Spirit and Opportunity landed on Mars and set about exploring, returning more than 100,000 images. They've also conducted geological tests on samples of rocks and soil. In 2009, the rovers uncovered evidence of water on Mars.

Engineers designed the rovers to run for just a few months, but they surprised everyone by lasting for years. In 2010, Spirit became trapped in sand (photo). Opportunity was still going strong in late 2014.

Voyager 1 and 2

Launched in 1977, Voyager 1 and 2 are still flying through space on a mission to explore the outer limits of our solar system. Along the way, the twin space probes took time to study the outer planets. Voyager 1 flew past Jupiter and Saturn, sending back images. Then the probe continued its journey deeper into space. It has now traveled more than 10.5 billion miles and is the farthest man-made object from Earth.

Voyager 2 took a grand tour of the outer solar system, visiting Jupiter, Uranus, and Neptune. It is set to enter interstellar space in 2015.

Each spacecraft carries a disk (photo, right) that contains images and sounds from Earth, including greetings in 55 languages to any life-form it may meet.

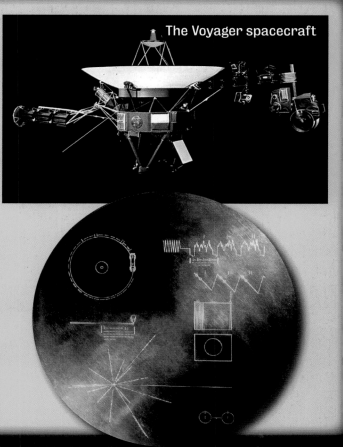

The Voyager spacecraft

New Horizons

On its journey to Pluto, the spacecraft New Horizons sailed past Jupiter in 2007, one year after it rocketed into space. The probe sent back images never before seen, such as lightning near Jupiter's poles and huge clumps of matter racing past the planet's rings. New Horizons is expected to reach Pluto by 2015.

This drawing shows New Horizons.

CHAPTER ② Weather & Climate

WHAT Is the Driest Place on Earth?

Arica, a city in Chile, in South America, once went 14 years without a single drop of rain. The average amount of precipitation that falls is a measly 0.03 inch. Arica is located in the world's driest desert—the Atacama.

The desert covers more than 600 miles. In this desolate area, you won't see plants or animals, just vast stretches of empty land. One region has soil that is similar to the kind found on Mars. In fact, sci-fi directors sometimes film in the Atacama.

You can see snow-capped Andes Mountains from the bone-dry Atacama Desert.

Weather is what it's like outside from day to day. Climate is weather over a long period of time. Check out both climate and weather facts on these pages.

CHILE

Plants in the Atacama Desert get the water they need by taking in moisture from fog.

Even though the Atacama Desert is such a harsh environment, there are towns and farms. How do people survive? Some communities transported water by truck, but that was very expensive. Today, they make use of a marine fog called *camanchaca* (ka-men-*chak*-a). Scientists found a way to collect the dense fog that forms on Chile's Pacific coast and drifts inland over the desert. People hang netting, which captures the water droplets in the fog. The droplets condense and drip into basins. The water is then piped to villages in the area. In the village of Chungungo, this system supplies the residents with more than 2,500 gallons of water each day.

Nets help collect water droplets in the fog.

WHAT Are the Most Extreme Daytime Temperatures Ever Recorded?

Brrrrr

July 2010, was an especially cold month in Antarctica. Using information from NASA satellites, scientists learned the thermometer dipped to −135.8°F, the lowest temperature ever recorded.

Hot Spot

Death Valley in California tops the heat charts. On July 10, 1913, the temperature reached a scorching 134°F, the hottest air-temperature ever recorded on Earth. During July, Death Valley has an average daily high of 115°F. At night, it cools down to a practically chilly 87°F!

WHAT Are Some Weather Myths?

It can't snow when the temperature is above freezing.

It can, if conditions are just right. Snowflakes form high up in the atmosphere whenever the temperature is at or below freezing. If, as they fall, they hit air that is above freezing, the flakes will start to melt. If the air is dry enough, the melting liquid cools the air surrounding the flakes (in the same way that sweating cools down our skin) and keeps the snowflakes from melting completely.

Lightning never strikes the same place twice.

Some places get hit again and again, especially if it's an object that's tall or is in an isolated setting, such as a lone tree in a field. The Empire State Building in New York City is hit more than 20 times a year.

A raindrop is shaped like a tear.

Raindrops start out as round droplets. As they fall, small raindrops under 0.03 inch stay round. Larger ones take on the shape of a hamburger bun, flat on the bottom and curved on top. Really large raindrops, those more than 0.17 inch in diameter, break apart and form two smaller drops. Tiny raindrops keep their round shape thanks to surface tension, the water's "skin" that makes molecules stick together. Larger drops, though, fall at a greater speed, so air pressure pushes against the base of the drop causing it to flatten.

WHAT Are the Northern Lights?

The areas around the Arctic Circle and the North Pole are the best viewing spots for one of nature's most spectacular light shows, the aurora borealis (ah-*roar*-uh bore-ee-*al*-is) or Northern Lights. Dazzling lights flicker and shift across the sky. Beginning as a sliver-green arc, this curtain of light ripples across the sky flickering, glowing, and shifting in shades of green, yellow, pink, red, blue, and purple.

What causes this fantastic display? The answer begins with the sun. Solar flare explosions shoot off particles of electrons and protons, some of which are carried away by solar wind. Traveling at speeds of more than 600,000 miles per hour, some of the particles eventually reach Earth. The Earth's magnetic fields tug at the energy-charged particles, pulling them into our planet's atmosphere. There they meet up with the main gases in our atmosphere, oxygen and nitrogen. The collision causes the gases to light up and glow in a profusion of color.

Visitors of Denali National Park, in Alaska, are occasionally treated to light shows.

The crew aboard the International Space Station took this picture of the aurora borealis.

The South Pole has its own light display. However, the aurora australis usually appears over unpopulated areas so few people ever get to see it. This photo was taken from space.

WHAT Is a Monsoon?

Which way does the wind blow? In India and much of Asia, the answer determines whether the land will be wet or dry. In winter, northeasterly winds bring warm, dry air for about six months. Then, around May, the wind pattern shifts, and moist southwesterly winds from the Indian Ocean cause heavy rains that drench the land. The heavy storms last six months before the dry air returns.

A monsoon, then, is a wind pattern that reverses with the seasons. There are two kinds of monsoons, dry and wet, and both can be extremely dangerous, although in very different ways.

Wet and Dry

During the wet monsoon, heavy rains sweep the land, causing flooding and landslides. In parts of India, rain dumps more than 400 inches of water. Although the wet monsoon can cause much damage, people need the rains to live. Without the storms, which bring as much as 90% of rainfall in a year, crops would die and people would go hungry.

When the winds shift again, the dry season returns. The land becomes parched. Heat waves and droughts are common.

Rickshaws and people wade through the flooded streets of a town in India.

WHAT'S More...

● Monsoon comes from the Arabic word mausim, meaning "season."

● Although monsoons are worse in Asia, other parts of the world also get these seasonal winds. Monsoons occur over large areas of land from Australia to the Caribbean Sea.

In 2011, Pakistan was affected by heavy flooding due to monsoons.

PAKISTAN

INDIA

INDIAN OCEAN

Too Much Rain

Cherrapunji, India, is one of the wettest places on Earth, yet it can go months without rainfall. During the dry monsoon season, villagers struggle to find drinkable water. Once the rainy season comes, Cherrapunji is drenched. The town averages 463 inches a year. One year, more than 900 inches of rain fell, almost all of it during the rainy season.

A man points to his damaged cotton crop. When the dry season returns after a monsoon, it can cause further damage to crops.

WHAT Is Acid Rain?

Most people think that rain is pure, clean water. But even clean rain contains some acid, though not enough to cause harm.

Acid rain, however, has way more acid than clean rain. In fact, some drops are almost as acidic as vinegar. Acid rain doesn't even have to be rain. It can be any precipitation, such as snow, sleet, or fog, that has unusually high amounts of acid.

Rain Pollution

Acid rain is caused by air pollution. The coal, oil, and natural gas we burn to run power plants, factories, homes, and vehicles, release gases into the air. Two in particular, sulfur dioxide and nitrogen oxide, are especially dangerous, at least when they combine with water vapor to become sulfuric acid or nitric acid.

Acid rain damages the environment, washing away nutrients in soil. It can kill fish and other marine life. Acid rain even harms buildings as it dissolves minerals in stone.

Good News

The good news is that efforts to combat acid rain are working. In 1990, the Clean Air Act required power plants to reduce the amount of sulfur dioxide they released into the atmosphere. Today, pollution levels are lower. Lakes that were once too acidic for fish are now teeming with life. Forests are coming back as well. But the work is far from over and more efforts will be needed to help reduce acid rain even further.

Acid rain killed many of the trees in this forest.

Buildings and statues, like those to the left, show signs of corrosion due to acid rain.

The pH Scale

Scientists measure acidity on a pH scale that goes from zero all the way up to 14. The stronger the acid, the lower its pH. Battery acid, for instance, is 0 on the scale. Tomato juice is 5. A solution that measures 7, such as distilled water, is right in the middle. It isn't acid at all. Neither is it alkaline, the opposite of acid. Liquid drain cleaner, an alkaline, tops the scale at 14.

Unpolluted rain has a pH rating of 5.6, just a bit more than the amount found in a banana. To be considered acid rain, the water must measure 5 or less on the scale.

A scientist collects a stream sample to determine the effects of acid rain.

WHAT Is the Northeast Passage?

Adolf Erik Nordenskiold

Who doesn't love a shortcut? For centuries people in Russia looked for a northern route from the Atlantic to the Pacific Ocean. The obvious way was to travel by sea along the northern coast of Russia. Unfortunately, this "climate-controlled" path lies in frigid Arctic waters and is frozen solid much of the year. It wasn't until 1878 that Adolf Erik Nordenskiold, a Finnish-Swedish explorer, made the first successful crossing through what is known as the Northeast Passage.

The passage is a shipping lane that runs from the North Pacific Ocean through the Bering Strait and the Arctic Ocean to the North Atlantic Ocean and Europe (see map). The route gave traders a shortcut between Europe and Asia. It shaved thousands of miles off the usual route through the Suez Canal in Egypt. The trouble was that ships could never make it through the passage in winter. Even during the summer months, floating ice made trips too dangerous for regular travel.

Icebreakers Pave the Way

Now, that's beginning to change. Global warming is shrinking the ice in the Arctic, and this is opening new lanes in the Northeast Passage. Ships still can't sail during winter months without the help of icebreakers. During summer, though, routes near the shore are becoming increasingly ice-free and more ships are passing through. Commercial shippers save money on these shorter trips because they spend much less on fuel.

Icebreakers are used to open sea lanes in the Northeast Passage.

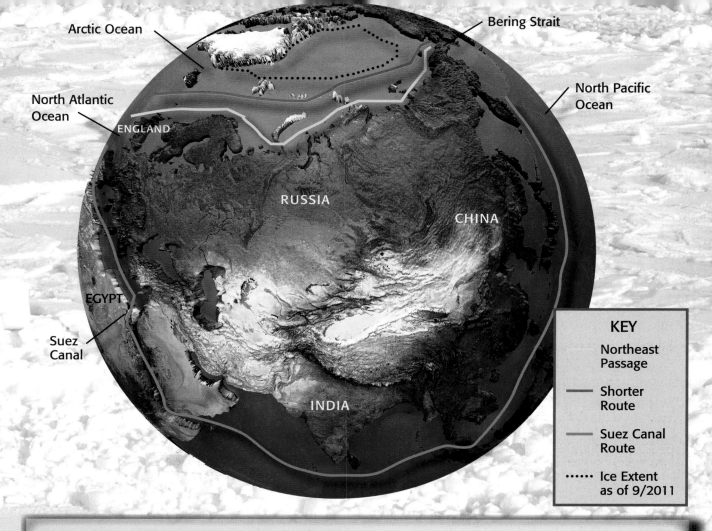

Arctic Ocean

Bering Strait

North Atlantic Ocean

North Pacific Ocean

ENGLAND

RUSSIA

CHINA

EGYPT

Suez Canal

INDIA

KEY

Northeast Passage

Shorter Route

Suez Canal Route

Ice Extent as of 9/2011

What Is Global Warming?

The Earth's average temperature is gradually rising. Year by year it is heating up. By 2100, many scientists predict that our planet's overall temperature will be from 2°F to 11.5°F higher than it is today. That might not sound like much, but only a difference of 9°F separates our time from the Ice Age.

Why is Earth getting hotter? Many scientists think burning fossil fuels, such as gasoline and coal, are to blame. The fuels give off carbon dioxide which rises into the atmosphere. This traps the sun's heat so it can't escape back into space. Global warming disrupts the climate and its weather patterns.

WHAT Is a Dust Devil?

It's a clear, sunny day with no clouds in the sky. Suddenly you spot a swirling column of air headed toward you. Is it a tornado? No, it's a dust devil, a whirlwind that you can see because it picks up dust and other debris from the ground.

Compared to tornadoes, dust devils are small, usually 10 to 15 feet around and from 100 to 400 feet high. Unlike most tornadoes, a dust devil lasts about a minute or so, with wind speeds under 50 miles per hour. Every once in a while, a more powerful dust devil forms. The largest can reach 300 feet across, last up to an hour, and travel at 60 miles per hour. Occasionally, dust devils can cause damage and injury.

Desert Dust Devils

Dust devils most often form in deserts and other wide-open places where the ground heats up until it is very hot. If this hot air rises and meets cooler air, the air may start to spin faster and faster. A dust devil will form if light winds tilt spinning air upright. Once vertical, the dust devil takes off, careening across the landscape. As more hot air feeds into the bottom of the whirlwind, the dust devil grows larger and spins faster. As soon as cooler air is sucked inside, the dust devil collapses.

WHAT'S More...

After Mount St. Helens erupted in 1980, people could see hundreds of sand devils that had formed from volcanic ash spin across the bare landscape.

Comparing Tornadoes and Dust Devils

TORNADO	DUST DEVIL
forms from thunderclouds	forms from the ground up
forms over wooded or plains area	forms over deserts
can be up to 2,000 feet high	can be up to 400 feet high
can spin up to 250 miles per hour	can spin up to 60 miles per hour
rotates counter-clockwise	rotates clockwise
lasts from 10 minutes up to an hour	lasts a few minutes

Martian Dust Devils

Dust devils swirl across the Red Planet, too, and they form there the same way they do on Earth. The Martian whirlwinds, though, are much, much larger than any on our planet—up to 50 times as wide and more than two miles high. Because dust devils are common on Mars, they could damage expensive equipment on NASA probes there. So far, this hasn't been a problem. Both the Spirit and Opportunity rovers on Mars met up with dust devils and came away with their solar panels cleaned! This greatly increased their power levels and extended the robots' usefulness.

WHAT Is an Anemometer?

The anemometer is a handy instrument used to measure wind speed. There are many kinds, but the simplest is the cup anemometer, invented in 1846 by John Thomas Romney Robinson, an Irish astronomer and meteorologist. This type of anemometer has four arms attached to the top of a pole. At the end of each arm is a cup, positioned to catch the wind. When the wind blows, the cups spin around the pole. Modern anemometers have an electrical device that records the cups' revolutions and calculates wind speed.

Other Types of Anemometers

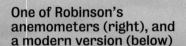

A windmill anemometer (left) gives the wind's direction, as well as its speed. An ultrasound anemometer (right) uses sound waves to determine wind speed.

Laser Doppler anemometers work by figuring out how much light from a laser beam is reflected off moving particles of air.

One of Robinson's anemometers (right), and a modern version (below)

TRY IT!

Make an Anemometer

What You Need

- 2 strips of cardboard, 1 inch x 12 inches
- stapler
- 4 aluminum foil baking cups
- sharpened pencil with an eraser
- permanent colored markers and/or stickers
- lump of clay, flattened at base
- push pin
- watch with a second hand

What to Do

1. Cross the cardboard strips in the shape of an X and staple at the center.

2. Decorate one of the baking cups with markers and/or stickers so that it stands out from the others.

3. Staple the cups to the cardboard frame, as shown. Make sure the open ends all face the same direction.

4. Push the sharp end of the pencil into the clay. Push the pin through the center of the cardboard frame and into the pencil's eraser.

5. Take your anemometer outside on a windy day and secure it on a flat surface. Record the number of revolutions it makes per minute by counting the decorated cup each time it passes you.

Note: While your model anemometer can't give you an exact wind speed, you can see how fast the wind is blowing by observing how rapidly the cups are turning.

WHAT If You Run into a Bear in the Wild?

If you are hiking or camping in bear country, let your wild neighbors know you're there. Make plenty of noise so that a bear will hear you coming and stay out of your way. Don't set up camp near hiking trails. Bears use them just like people do. Finally, food attracts bears. Keep supplies away from your campsite and hang food from a rope between two trees. Clean your site after meals. Bears are excellent sniffers and will track down leftovers, so burn any garbage. And remember: Never go hiking or camping without an adult.

If You Do Run into a Bear . . .

Stay calm and it's likely the bear will leave. Most bears attack only to protect their territory, food, or their cubs. If the bear follows, stop. Do not run. Curl up in a ball, and don't move. In most cases, the bear will leave when it no longer sees you as a threat.

Reading a Bear

A bear's body language can give you valuable clues about its mood. If the bear is swaying its head, clacking its teeth, and huffing, watch out! It is upset and likely to attack. Another sign of an angry bear is when its ears are pressed flat and its head is lowered. A bear standing on its hind legs is usually curious and just trying to get a better look or smell.

Watch Out!

What's Up?

What would you do if you came face to face with a wild animal, or were forced to go without food and water? Chances are excellent that these events won't happen, but just in case, here's how to be prepared.

WHAT If You Come Across a Snake?

Snakes are found everywhere. You might come across one in a forest, in the tropics, in the desert, or even in your backyard. Most snakes are harmless—to humans at least. But some species have glands that produce a poisonous venom that they inject to kill prey. They also use it in self-defense. If you step on a snake or walk too close to one, it will most likely strike out and attack. That's why it's important to follow these safety rules.

○ Don't pick up or touch any snake unless you are 100% sure it isn't venomous.

○ Wear boots and long pants if you are walking through tall grass or places where snakes might hide. It's also a good idea to carry a stick and pound the ground with it to let snakes know you're passing through.

○ Don't place your hands in cracks in stone walls or logs without first checking them for snakes.

○ Set up your campsite in a clearing, far away from trees, grass, and boulders.

Snakes to Avoid

Eastern Diamondback Rattlesnake North America's most dangerous snake, this rattlesnake can reach 96 inches. You'll find it in the southeastern United States.

Cottonmouth These aggressive snakes are often spotted sunning themselves near water. They are found in the southeastern United States.

Coral Snake With their bright bands of red, yellow, and black, coral snakes are easy to identify. You'll find them in the lower southern states, as well as in Arizona and New Mexico.

Sidewinder Although their venom is not as toxic as some other snakes, sidewinders are dangerous and a bite from one will hurt—a lot. These super-fast snakes live in the sandy deserts of the southwestern United States.

WHAT If You Get Lost While Hiking?

No one likes to get lost, especially when you're in the wilderness. That's why it is important to go hiking with a grown-up and to always let someone know where you are and what time to expect you back. Sometimes, though, even the best plans go wrong and you lose your way. Follow these tips, and you'll be out of the woods in no time.

Stay Put. Once you realize you're lost, the number one rule is to stay put. Don't wander about. You'll only make it harder for people to find you.

Take Cover. If it's cool, stay as warm and as dry as possible. If it's hot, you'll need to cool off. Stay in the shade and don't move around.

Make Noise. Make it easy for people to find you. Carry a whistle and a bright bandana so you can be more easily seen and heard. Wave your bandana and blow your whistle three times every few minutes. If you don't have a bandana or a whistle, alternately wave your hands and pound two rocks together.

Take a Snack. Always take a snack and water with you. Don't eat any food you find growing in the wild.

Your Outdoor Survival Kit

hat

flashlight

whistle

extra batteries

compass

snacks

water

bandana

GPS

WHAT Is the Lowest Body Temperature a Person Has Survived?

Anna Bagenholm, a Swedish doctor, went skiing one winter day in 1999, never imagining she'd end up in medical textbooks. While skiing, Bagenholm tumbled into an icy stream and became trapped under a thick layer of ice. With her head and upper body in freezing water, she found an air pocket and managed to hang on for the 80 minutes it took for rescue workers to free her. By the time she reached a hospital, she had no heartbeat and her temperature was 56.7°F—that's 42°F lower than normal. The doctor didn't think she would live.

Luckily, Bagenholm did live because her body cooled way down before her heart stopped. With a much slower metabolism, her cells didn't need as much oxygen. She holds the record for being the only person to survive such a low body temperature. Today, Bagenholm is once again working—and skiing.

Bagenholm was found in the mountains near the town of Narvik, Norway.

When Is HOT, TOO HOT?

As temperatures climb higher and the humidity rises, your body has to work harder to cool down. Sometimes, though, a body makes or takes in too much heat and can't cool down quickly enough. If the body's temperature goes above 105°F, a condition known as heat stroke occurs. Symptoms include hot, dry skin, a rapid pulse, headache, and vomiting. Sweating, the body's natural cooling system, stops completely.

The best way to get over heat stroke is to find a place with air conditioning and bathe in cool water. If you are out in nature, find shade and use water to cool off.

WHAT Is the Longest a Person Can Survive Without Water?

If you've ever played a sport in really hot weather, you know how quickly you lose water through sweating. The human body also loses water through urine and poop. This water must be replaced. Water regulates our body temperature, flushes out waste products, and helps carry nutrients and oxygen to our cells. That's why doctors recommend that people drink at least eight cups of water a day. If you are very active or if the weather is very hot, you need to drink more.

So how long can people survive without water? If they are healthy adults and the weather is mild, humans can go without water for three to eight days. Under extreme conditions, when temperatures are high, a person might survive two days.

Dehydration

When people don't have enough water in their bodies, they become dehydrated. At first the signs are mild. Your body won't produce as much saliva and urine. If dehydration continues, your mouth becomes dry and your heart beats faster. With severe dehydration, your body produces no urine at all.

WHAT'S More...

People and horses are among the few creatures that sweat. Most mammals cool off by panting. Dogs and cats have sweat glands on the pads of their feet and nowhere else.

What Is the Longest a Person Can Survive Without Food?

While no one can last long without H_2O, a healthy person can go up to two months without eating. The human body stores energy in the form of fat, so the chunkier a person is, the longer he or she will survive. As the stores of fat are depleted, the body starts to get weaker.

Don't Try This At Home!

David Blaine, the magician, went 44 days in 2003 without a bite to eat. And he did so suspended inside a clear plastic box dangling over the Thames River in England (photo, right). When his stunt ended, he had lost 54 pounds.

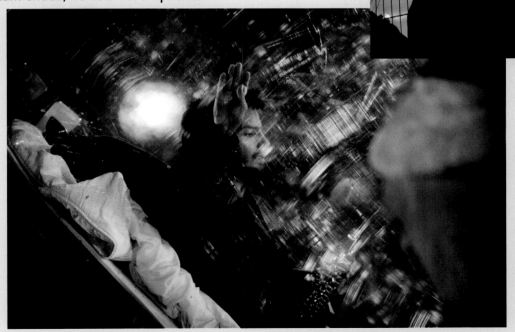

David Blaine waits to leave his box after going without food for 44 days. He did drink plenty of water, however.

WHAT Is the Deepest a Person Has Dived?

One of the world's most extreme and dangerous sports, free-diving, is an activity in which competitors take a single breath before diving underwater. There are different types of free-dive competitions, some taking place in pools and others in the ocean. Of all of them, No-Limit is the one that lets a diver go the deepest.

In No-Limit, a diver rides a weighted "sled" down to the ocean's depths. In 2012, Austrian Herbert Nitsch set the world record for the deepest No-Limit free dive. On his sled, Nitsch dove an amazing 830.8 feet—the length of a 76-story building—in ocean waters. He completed the dive on one gulp of air, holding his breath for more than four minutes.

How Do They Do It?

What makes it possible for a human to dive so deep? It's something that all warm-blooded creatures share, called the mammalian diving reflex. The response is triggered once the face is submerged in cold water. First, the heartbeat slows. As the body dives deeper, the pressure of all that water

makes the blood in the limbs withdraw, forcing it into the chest and to vital organs, such as the heart. As this takes place, the lungs become smaller and smaller until they are the size of lemons. The shrunken lungs can now work on less oxygen.

And the Winner for Deepest Animal Diver Is...

Don't hold your breath! The **sperm whale** has the honor of deepest air-breathing animal, diving to depths of 6,500 feet. Runners up include the Cuvier's beaked whale at 6,200 feet, the elephant seal at 5,000 feet, and the leatherback turtle at 4,200 feet.

Sylvia Earle (right) explores the ocean's depths.

Strolling on the Ocean Floor

Marine biologist Sylvia Earle set a world record in 1979 when, after descending 1,250 feet in a tiny submarine, she left the underwater vehicle and walked across the ocean floor. Earle, wearing a special pressurized diving suit and breathing through an oxygen tank, walked on the sea bottom for more than two hours, marveling at the strange creatures she saw there.

Glossary

acid rain precipitation that has high acidity because of being mixed with pollutants

air pressure the weight of the atmosphere that pushes down on people and objects

alkaline having a pH level above seven; the opposite of acidic

anemometer an instrument used to measure wind speed

Antarctica the ice-covered continent around the South Pole

Arctic the area around the North Pole

asteroid rocks, some the size of small planets, that orbit between Mars and Jupiter

atmosphere the envelope of gases around the Earth

camanchaca heavy fog that forms in the Atacama Desert and moves inland

cells the basic structure of all living things

climate weather conditions in one place over a long period of time

coma a thin cloud that surrounds a comet, made up from its heated gases and dust; a comet's coma can extend for millions of miles

comet a large chunk of rock surrounded by frozen gas and ice that orbits the sun

dark energy a form of energy that astronomers believe is responsible for the universe expanding at an increasing rate

dark matter an invisible form of matter that astronomers believe affects gravitational forces in the universe

dust devil a small whirlwind that raises a column of dust and debris

electron a tiny particle that moves around the nucleus of an atom

fossil fuels fuels, such as oil and coal, that are created by plant and animal matter over millions of years

gland a cell or group of cells that produces a substance that a body uses or gets rid of

global warming an increase in the average temperature of the Earth

gravity the force of attraction between two objects

hypergiant a star even more massive than a supergiant, hypergiant has a diameter that is 100 to 2,100 times the size of the sun's, and is extremely bright

lunar eclipse an eclipse in which the moon passes through the umbra of the Earth's shadow

magnetic fields the lines of force surrounding the sun and the planets, generated by electrical currents

mammal a warm-blooded vertebrate (having a backbone) that has hair or fur; mammals feed milk to their young.

mammalian diving reflex a reflex that allows mammals to stay underwater for long periods of time by slowing down the body's metabolism and compressing the lungs

marine biologist a scientist who studies ocean life

metabolism all the chemical processes that take place within a living organism that are necessary to sustain life

meteorite a mass of stone or metal that has fallen from space

meteorologist a scientist who studies the climate and weather

molecule the smallest part of a substance, made up of one or more atoms

monsoon a wind that changes direction with the seasons, especially the seasonal wind of India and southern Asia

nutrient a substance that an organism needs to live and grow

orbit the path one body takes around another, such as the path of the Earth around the sun

penumbra the outer, partially lighted shadow that surrounds the complete shadow (umbra) of a heavenly body during an eclipse

pH a number that expresses whether a solution is an acid or a base; a pH of 7 is neutral

pollution the contamination of air, water, or soil by harmful substances

precipitation rain, snow, or hail

proton a stable particle in the nucleus of an atom

radiation electromagnetic energy that moves in the form of waves

satellite a natural or manmade object that revolves around a planet

solar eclipse an eclipse in which the sun is obscured by the moon

space probe an unmanned spacecraft designed to explore the solar system and send information back to Earth

species a group of similar organisms

supergiant a star at least 100 times the sun's diameter and much brighter

supernova the explosion of a star

territorial defending one's land or territory

tornado a dark, funnel-shaped cloud made of fast-spinning air

umbra the darkest part of a shadow, cast by one heavenly body on another

vacuum a space completely free of matter or air

venom a poisonous substance produced by certain snakes and insects, usually given off in a bite or sting

Index